Extreme Plight
Americans On The Line

Copyright © 2012
by
David E. Robinson

Edition, October 2012

Maine-Patriot.com
3 Linnell Circle
Brunswick, Maine 04011

http://maine-patriot.com

Extreme Plight
Americans On The Line
Contents

Extreme Plight

The penalty of Treason is death.

Extreme Plight

Introduction

Any Judge, Government Agent, or Bureaucrat Who Has Sworn to Uphold the Constitution for the United States, Who is Violating that Oath, is Guilty of Treason. The penalty for Treason is death.

"You are weighed in the balance and are found wanting." — Daniel 5:27

"Woe, unto you lawyers! for ye have taken away the key to knowledge; ye entered [the Kingdom of God] not in yourselves, and them that were entering in ye [have] hindered." — Luke 11:52

Extreme Plight

1
The Legal Fraud
perpertrated on all Americans

Let's get right to the point.

The courts only recognize two classes of people in the United States today, **DEBTORS AND CREDITORS**

The concept of **DEBTORS AND CREDITORS** is very important for you to understand.

Every legal action where you are brought before the court — traffic ticket, property dispute or permits, income tax, credit cards, bank loans, or anything else they might dream up to charge you of, where you find yourself in front of a court — is in an **EQUITY COURT**, administering *commercial law,* with a ***debtor/creditor law*** as the controlling law.

We have an equity court, today, but not the equity court referred to in the Constitution of the U.S.; or in any of the legal documents prior to 1938.

All of the courts of this once great land have been changed, starting with the Supreme Court decision in ***Erie Rail Road v. Thompkins,*** 304 U.S 64 (1938).

Extreme Plight

2

U.S. Inc. Goes To Geneva; 1930's

In order for you to understand just how this fraud works, you need to know the history of its inception.

From 1928 to 1932 five years of Geneva Conventions took place. The nations of the world met in Geneva, Switzerland for 5 continuous years, to set up what became the general Policy of all the participating countries.

During the year 1930, the United States, Great Britain, France, Germany, Italy, Spain, Portugal, etc., all declared bankruptcy.

If you try to look up the 1930 minutes, you will not find them because they don't publish this particular volume. The 1930 volume which contains the minutes of what happened has been pulled out of circulation, or is hidden in the library and is very hard to find. This volume contains the evidence of the bankruptcy.

They stopped meeting in Geneva, in 1932, when Franklin Roosevelt came into power as President of the United States. Roosevelt's job was to establish and administer the bankruptcy that had been declared earlier, in 1930.

The corporate government needed a key Supreme Court decision on the record to set the stage for recognizing, implementing, and administering the bankruptcy.

This doesn't mean that the bankruptcy wasn't implemented *before* the 1938 *Erie Railroad v. Thompkins* decision. The bankruptcy started in 1930-1931.

The bankruptcy openly began when Roosevelt was sworn into office in January, 1933. He started the bankruptcy right away, with "The Banking Holiday", and proceeded to pull all gold out of circulation.

This was the beginning of the Public Policy of the United States for the bankruptcy.

3
Roosevelt Stacks the Supreme Court

Between 1933 and 1938, there was a big fight between Roosevelt and the Justices of the Supreme Court. Roosevelt tried to stack the Supreme Court with a bunch of his pals.

Roosevelt tried to enlarge the number of Justices and he tried to change the slant of the Justices. The corporate United States had to have a Supreme Court case that would support its bankruptcy problem.

There was much resistance to Roosevelt's court stacking efforts. Some of the Justices tried to warn us people that Roosevelt was tampering with the law and with the courts.

Roosevelt was trying to make sure that prior decisions of the court were overturned. He was trying to bring in a new order, a new precedent for the law of the land.

Extreme Plight

4
The "Mother Corporation"
Goes Bankrupt

A bankruptcy case was needed on the books to legitimize the fact that the corporate United States (U.S. inc.) had declared bankruptcy!

This bankruptcy was effectuated by a compact that the several corporate states made with the corporate government (the corporate Capitol of the several corporate states).

This compact (of the Governors of the several corporate states) tied the several corporate states to corporate Washington, D.C. (the headquarters of the corporation named "The United States").

Since the United States Corporation, having established it headquarters within the District of Columbia, declared itself to be in the state of bankruptcy, it presumptively declared bankruptcy for all its subsidiaries who were effectively pledged corporate members (the corporate state governments of the Union).

The corporate state governments didn't need to vote on the bankruptcy. The bankruptcy became effective by reason of the Compact/Agreement between the corporate state governments and THE MOTHER CORPORATION.

The term "Mother Corporation" communicates the interconnected power of the corporate Federal government relative to her association of corporation States.

The States created the Federal Government, however, and let the Federal Government take control of her "Creators" the States.

The Federal Government has become an out of control beast for power. She has for her **trade names** the following: **United States**; **U.S.**; **U.S.A.**; **United States of America**; **Washington, D.C.**; **District of Columbia**; **Feds**; and **Federal Government.**

She has her own **U.S. Army**; **Navy**; **Air Force**; **Marines**; **Parks**; **Post Office**; etc.

Because she is claiming to be bankrupt, she freely gives her land, her personnel, and the money she steals from us Americans via the I.R.S. and her state corporations, to the United Nations and the International Bankers, as payment for her federal corporate debt.

The UN and the International Bankers use this money and services for various world wide projects including war. War is a very lucrative business for the bankers of the New World Order. Loans for destruction. Loans for re-construction. Loans for controlling the people on her world property.

5

U.S. Inc. Declares Bankruptcy

The corporate United States is the Head corporate member which met at Geneva, to decide for all of its corporate body members.

Corporate representatives of the corporate several states did not attend. If the states had had the power to declare bankruptcy, apart from Washington D.C., then the several states would have been represented at Geneva.

The several states of America were not represented at Geneva. Consequently, whatever Washington D.C. agree to at Geneva, passed onto the several corporate states, via compact, as a group, association, corporation, or as a club.

All of the several corporate states agreed to and declared bankruptcy as one corporate governing group in 1938.

The several states were represented in Geneva via the United States located in Washington, D.C.

The delegates of the corporate United States who attended the meetings, spoke for the several corporate states, as well as for the Mother corporation located in Washington, D.C. — the seat and headquarters of the Federal Corporate United States.

And, presto BANKRUPTCY was declared for all.

From 1930 to 1938 the states could not enact any law, or decide any case, that would go against the Federal Government. The case decision had to come down from the Federal level so that the states would rely on the Federal decision, and use these is decisions as justification for the bankruptcy policy within the states.

Uniform Commercial Code (UCC) Emerges as the Law of the Land.

http://www.law.cornell.edu/ucc/1/overview.html

By 1938 the corporate Federal Government had the bankruptcy case of record they had been looking for.

Now, the bankruptcy, that had been declared back in 1930, could be up-held and administered. This is why the Supreme Court had to be stacked and made corrupt from within.

The new players on the Supreme Court fully understood that they had to destroy all case law established prior to 1938.

The Federal Government had to have a case of record to destroy all precedence, all appearance, and even the statute of law itself, i.e., the Statutes at Large had to be expunged.

They finally got their case in *Erie Rail Road v. Thompkins*.

And right after that case, the *American Law Institute* and the *National Conference of Commissioners on Uniform State Laws,* began devising the Uniform Commercial Code (UCC) that is on our backs today.

The Code was originally approved by its sponsors and the American Bar Association in 1952, and was revised in

1958 to incorporate a number of changes that had been recommended by the New York Law Revision Commission and other agencies.

Subsequent amendments that were deemed desirable in the light of experience under the Code were approved by the Permanent Editorial Board in 1962 and 1966.

The above named groups and associations of private lawyers got together and started working on the Uniform Commercial Code (UCC). By the early 40's and during the war, this committee was working to form the UCC and get it ready to put on the market.

The UCC is the law merchant's code for administering the bankruptcy. The UCC is the new law of the land as far as the courts are concerned.

This Legal Committee of lawyers put everything under the UCC; Negotiable Instruments; Securities; Sales; Contracts and Agreements; the whole mess.

That's where the word "Uniform" comes from. It means uniform from state to state, and uniform with the District of Columbia. It doesn't mean you didn't have the uniform instrument laws on the books before this time. It means that the laws were not uniform from state to state.

By the middle 1960's, every state had passed the UCC into law. The states had no choice but to adopt the newly formed Uniform Commercial Code as the law of the land.

The states fully understood that they had to administer the bankruptcy. Washington D.C. adopted the Uniform Commercial Code in 1963, six weeks after Kennedy was killed.

Extreme Plight

6
The Lawyers Secret Oath

What was the effect and the significance of the Erie Rail Road v. Thompkins case decising of 1838?

Since the Erie decision, no cases are allowed to be cited that are prior to 1939. There can be no mixing of the old law with the new law.

The lawyers (who were members of the American Bar Association and were and are currently under and controlled by the Lawyer's Guild of Great Britian) created, formed and implemented the new bankruptcy law.

The American Bar Association is a franchise of the Laweyer's Guild of Great Britian.

Since the *Erie Rail Road v. Thompkins case,* the practice of law in the United States has never been the same.

Reports indicate that every lawyer existing and coming up must take a SECRET OATH to support the bankruptcy.

Not only do lawyers and judges promise to support the bankruptcy, they also promise to never reveal who the true *party of interest* (the real creditor) is in the bankruptcy proceedings.

This is where you can call them for not making an appearance in court. If the true party to the action fails to appear, there is no way for the defendant know the true

NATURE AND CAUSE OF THE ACTION in court.

You are never told the true NATURE AND THE CAUSE OF WHY YOU ARE IN FRONT OF THEIR COURT. The court is forbidden to give you that information.

If you question the true nature and cause of the case, the judge will say, *"It's not my job to tell you; and I can't give you legal advice from the bench. I suggest you hire a lawyer."*

Hire a Lawyer?

If you hire a lawyer, who is pledged not to reveal the true nature and cause of the action. How will you ever find out the true nature and cause? You won't!

If the true nature and cause of the action against you is revealed, it will expose the **real creditor** from whom this action and cause came. They will have to name the TRUE creditor.

The true creditor will have to state the nature and cause of the action. The true creditor will have to say, "It's a bankruptcy proceeding."

This declaration then opens the door for you to question, *"Who the hell are you? How did you get attached to my back and by what document did I promise to become a debtor to you?"*

In this country, the courts on every level from the justice of the peace all the way up, even into the International Law arena, called the World Court, are administrating the bankruptcy, and are pledged not to reveal who the true creditors really are, and how you personally became pledged as a party to the corporate debt of the United States.

What would really drive these people away, would be to compel the International Bankers to send a lawyer into the courtroom as the attorney for the true creditor (themselves — the International Bankers). Then have the attorney put into the record *the true nature and cause of the proceedings against you that day* — the international bankruptcy of the United States and the world.

The International Bankers notified the various countries of the world that they were in a state of bankruptcy, and that they had been taken over by the creditor/bankers, and that there was no choice, but for all these countries to declare bankruptcy.

If the countries didn't agree to declare bankruptcy, the bankers threatened to collapse their economies and put them back into a depression like the one from which they were just emerging. The bankers made an offer they couldn't refuse!

Extreme Plight

7
To Elaborate and Review

In 1930 there was a world wide depression. The bankers said, "Look. You can do it (recover) in either of two ways. The easy way, or the hard way. Accept the bankruptcy, and we'll let you out of the depression. If you don't, you're on your own."

All the countries agreed, because they realized that the International bankers had them by the throat. The countries agreed that over the next several years they would pass statutes and legislation for the implantation of the bankruptcy, in favor of the International bankers.

And they've been doing so ever since.

Now, the key bankers are allegedly the Rothschild family (and their agents) via Rockefeller and the non-federal Federal Reserve bankers.

The point is, there was an international bankruptcy and an international conspiracy to cover it up. A banking creditor made an offer that countries accepted to enable them to continue to function without a revolution, and to keep their politicians comfortably in place.

Under a delusion of solvency the countries continued to function while they were, in fact, bankrupt.

Extreme Plight

8
The Snare

The bankruptcy scheme is an extremely clever and diabolical plan. So how did they pull this scheme off?

These Foreign bankers simply devised ways to entice (con) you into declaring yourself a CITIZEN (or RESIDENT) of the corporate United States.

Remember the corporate United States is Bankrupt per public policy, and agreement.

After you had been tricked into claiming that you were a corporate CITIZEN of the corporate United States, you were given a Social Security Number, which ties you to certain meager "benefits" and "privileges" of the corporate United States.

Then, the bankers conned your employer to function as an unpaid tax collector, to con you into filling out their **W-4 intangible property gift forms** and **1040 voluntary agreements.** These slick paper agreement established your **"voluntary indebtedness"** to them, the banker creditors.

If at any time you decide to balk at this scheme because you don't like it, the **real creditor** never has to make an appearance in court, to list the true nature and cause of action being brought against you.

You end up dealing with an agency, which can conveniently claim immunity from prosecution because all it is doing (without your knowledge and consent) is administering the bankruptcy that the government agreed to, per the Geneva conventions.

The court system never lets you put the original creditor on the courtroom stand so you can ask him how he got attached to your back.

The system is set up in such a way that the TRUE CREDITOR IS PROTECTED and never has to make an appearance, and never has to answer any of your questions or produce documents.

Therefore, the true creditor never has to produce the law that gives him the right to pledge you (your body and labor) into indebtedness (bondage/servitude). Why? Because the Geneva agreement, in 1930, was done via treaty.

The bankruptcy was not done by legislation. The agreement came first, — signed in secrecy. THEN Congress began to pass legislation to fulfill the bankruptcy obligation that the treaty required.

Legislation passed by Congress was then and is thereby now bankruptcy legislation. When cases come before the courts, the courts can make decisions based on the new controlling bankruptcy law. It has nothing to do with Constitutional rights.

Now, any case brought in is under the new bankruptcy law and is not considered a true constitutional case. It is a bankruptcy case now as distinct from, but cleverly disguised as a constitutional case.

The members of the Supreme Court realized what was happening to them and the system of law. The court was being asked to perform in a creditor-debtor bankrupt proceeding for the benefit of the banker creditors.

Extreme Plight

9
The Fraud

The members of the Supreme Court said, in essence, *"NO. We will not give you a bankrupt proceeding decision that you can then enforce against everybody, a decision not only affecting corporate Washington D.C., but also the corporate state governments.*

This by the way is fraud.

It wouldn't be fraud if the corporate government of Washington D.C. and the corporate governments of the several states declared bankruptcy and then told the people about the bankruptcy.

Notice that "corporate government" doesn't mean you and me. You and I are not the corporate government. The corporate government is the corporate capital of the corporate state.

The government is a neutral government zone known as the *capitai ci,* the corporate state. The government is where the corporate state is. It is corporate headquarters. Just like corporate Washington D.C. is the seat of the corporate Federal Government.

The *capitai ci,* the corporate state, is the seat of the corporate state government.

If the corporate Federal Government and her subsidiary

corporate state governments want to join forces and declare bankruptcy that's not fraud. This is their corporate business.

However, it *is* fraud when those two corporate entities declare bankruptcy, but do not disclose to you and me, and every other American, that they have done so, declared bankruptcy.

Further they do not disclose that their intention is to get you and every other American in this country pledged to pay off their corporate debt to their corporate creditors. The corporate bankruptcy is the federal responsibility of the corporate state, not the responsibility of Americans, the people.

The public U.S. Inc. is separate and distinct from private Americans

"We the People" created and signed the contract/compact/agreement of by and for the Constitutional Corporation using the trade name the "united States of America" as a corporate entity (legal fiction) DISTINCT AND SEPARATE from Americans (the unenfranchised people of America).

The private natural American people did not create the corporation of the United States. The United States Inc. did not create the private natural American people.

America and Americans were in existence prior to the creation of the United States Corporation which located its U.S. headquarters in Washington, D.C.

Virginia state (state territory) gave land to the newly formed United States Corporation. Notice, here, we have a state giving something of value (contract consideration, land) to the United States.

The United States Corporation agreed in the Constitutional contract, to protect the states. Instead, because of their bankruptcy (Corporate U.S. Bankruptcy), this U.S. corporation has enslaved the people and the states by deception at the will of their foreign bankers with whom they have been doing business.

Our forefathers gave their lives and property to prevent our enslavement. Today, we are again enslaved.

Natural private American people have been tricked, deceived, and 'setup' to carry the perpetual corporate debt of the U.S. Inc. under bankruptcy laws.

Every time Americans appear in court, the corporate U.S. bankruptcy is being administered against them without their knowledge and lawful consent. This is FRAUD. All administrating of the corporate bankruptcy is done by "Public Policy" of by and for the Mother Corporation (U.S. Inc.).

11
The Mother Corporation's "Public Policy"

The corporate bankruptcy is carried out under the "corporate public policy" of the corporate Federal Government in corporate Washington, D.C.

The states use "state public policy" to carry out the "federal public policy" of Washington D.C. Public Policy and only public policy is being administered against you in the corporate courts today.

The public policy dictated by all the courts, from the smallest to the most powerful courts in the world, is public policy. This is why the people of other countries have also be enslaved into indebtedness. It has become public policy to have the people of other countries go into joint corporate debt. The people of other countries have been forced to promise to pay these debts, and they are being forced to pay off on those corporate debts.

Corporate Public Policy is the crux of the whole bankruptcy implementation. Corporate Public Policy is forever a Corporate Public Policy and the laws that have been passed since 1938 are all corporate public policy laws dealing only with corporate public policy.

Understand that U.S. corporate public policy is Not an American public policy. It's the public policy OF (belonging to) the corporate United States. The U.S. public policy of corporate bankruptcy is not OF (belonging to) the American Republic.

The 1938 *Erie Railroad v. Thompkins* case was a decision based upon public policy. All decisions at any level since then (1938) have been public policy decisions.

All statutes, rules, regulations, and procedures that have been passed, whether civil or criminal, whether federal or state, have been passed to implement the public policy of bankruptcy.

Ever since 1933, when F.D.R. came into office, F.D.R. brought in public policy. He established that it was the public policy of the government to call in all the gold. It was the public policy of the Government in Washington, D.C. (the Federal Government) to give our government assistance in paying its debt.

Public policy operates the same within the states. All Federal court decisions can only be handed down if the states agree with and support Federal public policy. The legal systems of the states must be compatible with the legal system of the Feds.

12
The Monkey Wrench

This is why, when common people like us go to court without being represented by a lawyer, we throw a monkey-wrench into the corporate administrative proceedings. Why? Because all public policy corporate lawyers are pledged to uphold public policy, which is the corporate administration of their corporate U.S. bankruptcy.

That's why you'll find stamped on many if not all our briefs, "THIS CASE IS NOT TO BE CITED IN ANY OTHER CASE AND IS NOT TO BE REPORTED IN ANY COURTS."

The reason for this notation is that when we go in to defend ourselves or file a claim we're not supporting the corporate bankruptcy administration procedure. The arguments we put forth predate 1938. We come in with Constitutional law, etc.

All these early cases support our rights not to be in bankruptcy. However, corporate court lawyers and judges have promised to give no judicial recognition of any case prior to 1938.

Extreme Plight

13
The International Bankers' Corporate Plantation U.S.A. Style

Before 1938, the law was Not a "public policy" law. All these old cases were not public policy law decided cases, as they are today. "Public policy" exists to administer the bankruptcy for the benefit of the banker creditors, to protect the banker creditor.

Corporate public policy allows the Creditor to say to the corporate legislatures, "I want a law passed requiring my debtors to wear seat belts. Why? Because I want to be able to milk my debtors for the longest period possible."

It doesn't behoove the creditor to allow his labor producing debtors to die at an average age of 30 years. What would happen to the bankers' lending, interest, penalties, repayment, etc. of the entire funding and lending process if the average American life span was only 30 years?

Why, the bankers would have to have 2-1/2 times the current consumer population to equal their current take. The bankers would need (instead of 250 million Americans) 600 million, or even more. Maybe the bankers would need 2 Billion Americans because the individual can't contract for debt until he/she is 18 or 21 years of age. Therefore, if the average life span is only a 30 year period, the creditor could collect on the debt for only 12 years.

Now, if the bankers can just get people to live an average of 70 years, you are talking a whopping 50 years of indebtedness for which they contract and for which they are forced to pay back with usury/interest.

With this situation, the banker creditor can now float loans worth 50 years of potential indebtedness, and its payoff with interest in the name of the people, instead of 9 to 12 years.

The creditors and their property and their people are well taken care of. The creditor doesn't want the population to decrease, per say, unless, it is convenient for the debtor to run up debts in another's name, and then liquidate that debtor or that group of debtor people.

14
The AIDS problem today

For example let's consider the AIDS problem today among the black people. What better group to inject AIDS into than the black people? Read the *Stracker Memorandum on AIDS* and the *World Health Organization* connection, that documents their tainted vaccination program in Africa and elsewhere.

Why not kill them off? Don't you understand that the blacks as a whole have absorbed all the debt that they can absorb? The blacks have reached the maximum of the debt that they can carry. In fact, they have gone over their limit to pay back.

They are now heavily into welfare, public housing, medicaid, medicare, food stamps, etc. The situation now is that instead of paying off the creditor, they have become a drain on the creditor.

The creditor must now pay them to live and take care of them. What creditor in his right mind wants to spend money on a bunch of people from whom he can't collect any revenue?

The corporate public policy of the corporate United States and the states, and the counties and of the cities, is that YOU must take care of these people. You must provide them with welfare, etc. Why?

Because when you, as a member of the corporate body politic, allow laws to be passed which says the minorities must be taken care of; the corporate legislature can *then* say that it has become "public policy" that the people want these people taken care of.

Therefore, when given the chance, the legislature can say the "public policy" is that the people want these blacks and poor whites to be taken care of and given a chance.

We must, therefore, raise taxes to fund all these benefits, privileges and opportunities. This is what these people need to make them socially, politically, and economically equal with every one else.

The legislatures have passed all kinds of statutes providing for high indebtedness and they float the indebtedness off your backs because you have never stepped forward to challenge them; to tell them that it is not your public policy to assume other people's debts.

On the contrary, all the court decisions coming out, indicate it is the corporate public policy and it is your willingness to support the corporate public policy to pay off these debts.

Remember, "public" means of and for the corporate Government. It does Not mean of and for private people. "Public" means corporate government; corporate government policy. When they talk about public debt, they are talking about corporate government debt and your *presumed pledge* against this corporate created debt.

15
The Real Estate Snare

How do they work this scheme in the area of real estate?

These bankers have made an agreement that it is corporate public policy that all land (property) be pledged to the creditor to satisfy the debt of the bankruptcy, which the creditor claims under bankruptcy.

They get away with this the same way they get away with any other case that is brought before the court, whether it's a traffic ticket, IRS claim, or whatever. Here is how it works.

You have signed legal instruments giving information and jurisdiction to the bankers through their agents. The instruments (forms) you signed include, but are not limited to the following:

social security registration, use of the social security number, IRS forms, driver license, traffic citation, jury duty, voter registration, using their address, zip code, U.S. postal service, a deed, a mortgage application, etc. etc.

The bankers then use those instruments (documents) under the Uniform Commercial Code (UCC) as contracts/agreements. These documents are considered to be *promissory contracts* wherein you promise to perform.

This scheme involves you, without you ever becoming directly in contact, or in contract with the true creditor. What's more, you are never informed as to who the true creditor is, and the true nature and cause of the paperwork, that you are filling out, is never divulged to you.

If you examine your real estate deed, you will find that you promised to pay taxes to the corporate government.

On property you originally acquired through a mortgage, you will notice that the bank never promised to pay taxes. You did.

The corporate government at all levels never promised to pay taxes to the creditor. You did. In tax and collection problems relating to real estate being enforced against you, you will notice that there is no mention in the mortgage or the deed stating the true nature and cause of the action.

Since you made the promise to perform, you get a bill every year for property taxes.

You don't realize that the only way they can bill you for taxes is through your own stupidity of AGREEING to pay the tax. You volunteered.

They took advantage of you, conning you into promising to pay property taxes. When they send you their bill, they are coming against you for the collection of the promise you made to the creditor.

Now, the creditor on the paperwork appears to be the local bank. The bank has loaned you "credit". The bank hasn't loaned you anything. It was not their credit to loan. This is why the bank can't loan credit.

There is a credit involved, but it is not the bank's credit. It's the International bankers' credit. The international bankers are loaning you their credit based upon the operation of their bankruptcy claim against you personally, as well as your property.

Now, let's say you are not aware of the remedies provided for you within the Uniform Commercial Code (UCC). The UCC allows you to dishonor the county's presentment of your tax bill.

You don't pay your tax bill. You just sit on it and don't do or say anything. A couple of years go by and all of a sudden you are being sent letters to pay up what is owed, or else in a certain period of time your property will be taken from you and put up for a tax sale.

Now here is what is interesting - If you don't pay your tax bill, and they contact you asking you to pay it and you don't pay it, they will declare you in default. Based on that default, as provided in the UCC, they sell your property for the tax (the rent).

However, the county never goes into court, to put into the record the identity of the real creditor. And the county does not state the *true nature and cause of the action* against you (a bankruptcy action disguised as a tax action). Why?

Because, under bankruptcy implementation, they have developed a legal procedure which is based upon YOUR PRESUMED PROMISE TO PAY. They don't have to come into the court to get a court order authorizing the sale of your property. Therefore, the real creditor never makes an appearance in court.

The reality is, you are denied any possibility of appearing in court to exercise your right to challenge the creditor; to ask if he became the creditor under "public policy"; to ask if it is under "public policy"; and just what is "public policy"?

How did you (as an international banker) become "creditor" to me, and to everyone else in this country (American people).

They don't want you to ask the real creditor (the International Bankers), to PRODUCE THE DOCUMENTS upon which your personal debt is established. If they were forced to go into court, they would have to produce the deed or mortgage showing you KNOWINGLY, WILLINGLY, and VOLUNTARILY promised to pay the corporate public debt.

You did Not KNOWINGLY, WILLINGLY, and VOLUNTARILY promise to pay any U.S. Corporate Bankruptcy obligation made way back in the 1930's. This rebuttal would, of course, expose their racket.

The fact is, that there was no debt connected to you until you unknowingly agreed to it through their deception and fraud. The deception, in a broader sense, permeates the educational system and the new age media, etc., to sell you on the idea that you are a statutory **"U.S. Citizen"** and **"Resident"** of the corporate United States. (INC.)

16
Your signature is your most valuable property

Your "property" is pledged, for the rest of your life, upon your signature, and your *promise to perform* is pledged into perpetual debt.

The bankers don't even bother to go to court. They leave it up to the corporate agencies to administer the corporate agencies' public policy.

It is the public policy of those agencies to bill you on your *promise to perform*. If you don't pay based on your *promise to perform,* they follow up with a notice of default, and give you one more chance to pay. Then they proceed to sell the property at a tax auction sale.

They never go to court or appear in court to back up their claim against you.

Did any of your government licensed and controlled teachers ever stress THAT YOUR SIGNATURE IS YOUR MOST VALUABLE PERSONAL PROPERTY? Did your government teachers ever tell you, that any time you sign any document, you should sign it **"without prejudice"** or with **"All Rights Reserved"** above your signature.

This means that you are reserving you God given unalienable (un-lien-able) rights (rights which cannot be liened or transferred) and all other rights for which your forefathers died.

The Corporate U.S. Government provides, or at least pretends to provide, for this reservation of rights under the Uniform Commercial Code (UCC) at 1-207 and 1-103.

You need more information in this area. It is not in the best interest of the United States Corporate "Public" schools to teach you about their bankruptcy proceedings, and how they have set the snare to COMPEL YOU INTO PAYING THEIR DEBT.

The Corporate "Public" schools are strictly designed for their Corporate citizens/subjects; i.e. the Corporate U.S. Public School citizens. Notice all their emphasis on "being a 'good' citizen".

Basically, all their teachers and their students are trained to produce labor and material in exchange for valueless paper called "money." It is not money; it functions "AS" money. Lawful money must be backed by something of value.

Bankers take your labor, services, and material (your homes, cars, farms, etc.) in exchange for their valueless corporate paper. This paper is backed only by the "full faith and confidence of the United States Government" (THE MOTHER CORPORATION).

I do not have faith or confidence in the U.S. BANKRUPT CORPORATE GOVERNMENT ADMINISTRATORS WHO HAVE PERVERTED THEIR CONSTITUTIONAL CHARTER, enslaving the sovereign American people into THEIR bankruptcy obligations. Their fraudulent money laundering process promotes your payment on the corporate government's bankruptcy debt, that is mathematically impossible to pay off.

You and your family are in continual financial bondage to the international bankers. They love it so!

Black's Law Dictionary 1990, defines "Money Changers" as: - "business of a banker... today handled by the international departments of banks."

Let's think for a moment, what did Christ do to the "Money Changers?" Oh, Yes, he severely interfered with their activity. Three days later Christ was crucified. Lincoln was killed for interfering with the money chargers too. Kennedy was slaughtered for interfering with the money changes.

Extreme Plight

17
My Brother's Case

In my brother's case, he was never in default as he never made the promise in the common law deed to pay taxes, therefore, the man who bought my brother's property is moving against him through an attorney who is claiming that my brother never redeemed the property.

The attorney had followed procedure by publishing the property tax notice in the newspaper for three printings. Now they show up in court to get the court to declare default. Then after a default judgment, the attorney's client has a legal right to the property.

So my brother comes in and challenges this action. The problem is, the man who bought the property, is trying to claim the property when in fact, he is not the original creditor. He is not the person who said my brother was in default or that he owed a tax in the first place.

Now, when my brother comes in and challenges the new buyer, the court rules that the new buyer is not required to produce any documents in support of his cause. The only documents they are required to produce are the documents related to the foreclosure procedure.

Do you understand? There is no court case where the true creditor has to make an appearance. You cannot question or challenge the true creditor.

When you do go to court, the person you are allowed to question is the person who bought the property. The buyer is not required to produce documents because the only one who would be required to do so, is the true creditor. Now you are in the position of fighting yourself in court.

This is a very clever way for the creditor to avoid the courts in order to settle the dispute for his claim against you. This is also very clever way to avoid naming the true claimant; the true plaintiff.

The true plaintiff is the international bankers. The international bankers claim they have a claim against my brother's property because my brother's property has been pledged by the state as collateral for the corporate debts under the bankruptcy to the international bankers.

Once my brother removed his property from their jurisdiction and venue, by claiming back all his rights, titles and interest, the only way that they would be able to stand a chance, would be for the original claimants (the international bankers) to make an appearance through their attorney, and for my brother to require their attorney to place in the record, a statement, identifying the true nature and cause for their actions.

The courts and the attorneys have cleverly avoided this process.

Remember, when you are dealing in bankruptcy, slight of hand, lies, and deception, you have to **protest to the head man in the action,** just like the Watergate tapes. Everybody tried to protect Nixon, the head dog.

It is the same in this bankruptcy scam, they all have to

protect the International Bankers. The proof that this is true is that: (1) My brother is now in front of the court of appeals, the attorney for the people who bought the property, has already said, the buyers should not be required to present the authority establishing the State of Maryland's authority to tax property and to collect these taxes; This statement is the tip-off for how they are attempting to protect the International Bankers.

Since the International Bankers never had to appear in court, they never were required to show where they got the right to pledge everybody's property into the corporate debt of the United States.

The buyer's attorney says his client should not have to produce anything, and this court should not demand that he has to produce. Guess what. The court will agree with the buyer's attorney. They don't have to do it. They have to protect everybody's butt.

The attorney never cited one case before 1953. The attorney put a lot of cases in his paperwork but nothing is cited before 1938. Most of the cites are since 1963, when the State of Maryland passed the UCC.

Most of the cites were in the 70's and 80's. A few cites were in the late 60's and one in the 50's. This lawyer knew what was going on. That's why, no matter what happens, someone in the court will stamp on the paperwork that "this case cannot be cited in other cases. This case is not to be reported in the legal reports."

Extreme Plight

18
The Cover-up

There was a deal struck, that if any person, who doesn't have a lawyer to bring his case before the courts, proves the fraud and speaks the truth about the fraud, the courts are compelled to not allow the case to be cited or published anywhere.

The courts cannot afford to have the case freely available in the public archives. This would be evidence of the fraud. This is why you can't (shouldn't) hire an attorney. An Attorney is compelled to uphold the fraud.

"Trust Me. I'm here to help you. I have the governments permission to practice law. I'm a Member of the Bar."

The attorney is there for one basic reason. To make sure that the bankruptcy scam (established by the corporate public policy of the corporate Federal Government) is upheld.

The lawyer's will cite no cases for you that will go against the bankruptcy in corporate public policy. Whatever the lawyer will do for you is a bunch of BULL. The lawyers have to support the bankruptcy and public policy, even at your expense. The lawyers can't go against the corporate Federal Government statutes which implement, protect and administer the bankruptcy.

For all cases cited, those in the U.S. Code or the state annotated code, or any other source, they only selected those cases that support the "public policy" of bankruptcy.

The legal system has to work this way. After the last 30 or 40 or 50 years of cases that have been decided based on upholding the bankruptcy, the legal system couldn't possibly allow someone to put in the record information and evidence to prove the fraud.

19
Blood in the Streets

Can you imagine how damaging it be, if they allowed your case to be cited in another case, or if they allowed the public to examine a copy of your brief, that discloses evidence of the fraud?

This exposure would render null and void everything for which they have worked so hard to attain. Wouldn't this exposure make the people mad? Wouldn't this exposure mean there would be blood running in the streets?

Especially in the cities where the poor people have been really taken by this diabolical system. What the court is concerned about is that a case that goes against the bankruptcy, never be cited, for if the bankruptcy is ever exposed, the people would go for their guns and shoot the SOB's.

Extreme Plight

20
Mr. Sweet's Case Disappeared!

There is a man, let's say his name is Sweet. He has been investigating corporate government activities for more than 12 years, on a full time basis. Now, let's look at a recent case that he won.

He went into court and defended *his common law lien* on his property, to be compatible with statutory law.

The judge said, "Since you presented me with a lien on your property, I will rule that the county is the owner of your property, with the condition that all liens be satisfied."

Sweet was very happy about the judgment. Sweet doesn't care if the county is the owner of the property because the county can't take the property for the next 90 years of the lien.

The county can't take the property away from him because of his *common law lien* on the property. Sweet is free to use it, rent it, sell it, whatever. If the county really wants the property, they have to satisfy the lien first.

But there is a problem regarding setting this precedent. Sweet went back a couple of weeks later and asked them to punch up his case number. Guess what? The case number had disappeared!

After the judge ruled that the county owned the property, subject to the lien, it became a case that goes against the public policy of corporate county bankruptcy.

Since Sweet placed a lien on his own property, he is the one who has to be paid off first - not the county! The county must satisfy the lien before the county is allowed to take possession of the property.

The property is probably not worth the price of the lien. This would not satisfy the true creditors, the International Bankers. If the county pays Sweet off first, the city has to place on their records a $75,000.00 deficit.

The true creditors wouldn't like that deficit. They certainly wouldn't like the fact that Sweet's clever maneuver had out foxed the foxes.

What if one hundred, two hundred, a thousand, or ten thousand, people in this state/republic would just put a **common law lien** on their property and then stopped paying property taxes, and then cited Sweet's case. It would set a precedent.

Let the county have the property as long as the judge makes the judgment "subject to existing liens." In this situation, the county would end up holding all this property but would have no use of it. No taxes. No rents. All deficient.

The banker creditors certainly don't want this scenario. The bankers don't want any cases administered except through the application of bankruptcy procedure. The bankers want your rights, privileges, and due process strictly administered by and through the corporate courts under their corporate public policy, international bankruptcy procedure.

The International Bankers and their UNREGISTERED FOREIGN AGENTS don't want any evidence on the record, showing how you can get out from under their grasp.

Any revenue collecting individual or agency such as the courts, judges, lawyers, law enforcement officers, and tax collectors who are attempting to take money from you, *as a private American,* must be registered as a foreign agent.

If they are not duly registered and properly identified, they are involved in EXTORTION AND TREASON *against private Americans.*

Extreme Plight

21

How Sweet It is!

As part of Sweet's maneuver, he filled out a financing statement using the UCC-1 form, whereby he put his wife and himself as debtors and creditors. Now, the legal situation is switched. The UCC-1 Financing Statement Sweet recorded with the state, shows Sweet and his wife as **parties of interest recorded with the state** rather than the presumption that the international bankers are parties of interest instead.

There is an office within each corporate state (Secretary of State) that handles the UCC-1 forms for personal property, and a county recorder's office who records the UCC-1 against real property.

Since Sweet is listed on corporate state records as **the debtor and the creditor** of his own property, his property can't be put up for collateral against any debts claimed by the bankers, in any way.

Now, the International Bankers, and their agents, cannot prove that Sweet's property is debt collateral belonging to the bank or the corporate county. The property is encumbered by Sweet's lien. Therefore, the property cannot be put up against any debt claims until it is no longer encumbered by Sweet's lien.

Sweet's property is now free and clear of all liens except

his. For all practical purposes, the property is now Sweet's, being unencumbered by any further demand for payment of taxes.

Sweet has not paid property taxes for many years. Sweet is now his own creditor, and his own debtor. Therefore, the International Bankers and the corporate county thieves are knocked out of the stealing process. How sweet it is! Congratulations to Mr. Sweet!

You may want to do it the same way too.

If you own property, get your deed and a common law lien, and fill out a UCC-1 Form. Then file it with the Secretary of State *for personal property,* and with the county recorder *for real property.*

This seems to be a good way for you to get out from under these foreign corporate International Bankers. The judges have to know what's going on. The only way their scheme can work is to have all the lawyers and judges pledge to uphold the corporate bankruptcy public policy.

The bankers just can't allow lawyers in a legal system who refuse to uphold the bankruptcy policy. These renegade lawyers would have to be quickly weeded out.

They certainly have a neat little scheme going on here in America. The Land of the *Fee* and the Home of the *Slave*.

22
Attention Law Student

I hope you're reading this book, Law Student. You said you wanted to be a lawyer. Well, I hope you're listening closely, because here is the legal system you're headed to serve, and serve you will.

You said you wanted to be a lawyer so you can find out what oath they're taking, in secret, behind closed doors in solemn preparation for the "business of the court" as judges and lawyers.

Now, you know the oath. The oath is simply to uphold the bankruptcy. If you want to be a lawyer and want to make a living as a lawyer, I can tell you this, they will weed you out at the very beginning, if you don't bring in your paperwork under the bankruptcy procedures.

If you try to defend your clients, and try to help your clients, they will get rid of you. The will pull your license. So you spend all that money and time going to school under the guise of helping people, and end up wasting your time. Without that license you can't go into a courtroom. I would think about this if I were you.

Extreme Plight

23
Traffic Citation

Regarding the UCC-1 Form, you can also file it against your car. Wouldn't it be a kick in the tail if you went into court for a traffic citation, where you had conditionally accepted the traffic citation by having signed **"Without Prejudice, UCC 1-308"** and sent in the traffic citation marked **"refused for cause without dishonor"**.

Now, let's say you are in front of the judge. The judge says, "What's this refusal for cause stuff all about?" The judge won't want any mention that the citation was issued under bankruptcy. He is afraid you'll mention the bankruptcy issue.

The reason you **"refused** [the traffic citation] **for cause without dishonor"** is that, *it was issued to you under bankruptcy corporate public policy.* He won't want get in to that, so when you get before the judge, just say, *"I have removed myself from the bankruptcy; my auto is no longer pledged as collateral against the debt."*

He may say, "Oh yeah? What are you talking about?"

That's when you hand him the UCC-1 Form you had filed with the state. *"This UCC-1 Form shows that I am the debtor and the creditor on my auto."*

Now what happened? The corporate county/state can't collect on the traffic citation debt instrument. Why? Because if they collect a $100.00 fine, they have to pay you the amount of the fine, because you're the creditor on the ticket. How sweet it is! You're the creditor of your property, are you not?

People have done this. There is no record, of course, no paper trail. Such cases are not cited. The corporate banker's agents, clerks, lawyers, judges, etc., take the information out of the record, as soon as you beat them at their own game.

24
The Lawyer's Guild Connection

The American Bar Association is a franchise of the Lawyer's Guild of Great Britain.

The American Bar Association is not primarily concerned with what happens in any case on the local level. However, when a case leaves the local level, by that, I mean the state court, city court, or the justice of the peace, or even the federal court, and goes to the appeals court, it appears that the American Bar Association takes notice of the case.

It seems that the American Bar Association has an agreement that any action brought on an appeal, must be reviewed by the American Bar Association.

If this is true, it would make sense. How else would the American Bar Association — a branch of the Lawyer's Guild of Great Britain, the legal arm of the Rothschild Dynasty — be able to monitor and administrate the corporate Bankruptcy.

It appears that the American Bar Association is compelled to review all appeals cases and to make certain any case brought under the common law, or the constitutional law, that would expose the bankruptcy, would be immediately stamped on the back that **"this case is not to be cited or published."**

I believe that this is the stamp origin and purpose of its message in such cases. The justice department may be able to do that in Washington, D.C., but I can't see where any judge or lawyer could have the authority to stamp or label a case as one not to be cited for future cases.

I think that is an official stamp from the American Bar Association.

25

The Bankruptcy Accounting System

Now, Joe Law Student, if your still attending classes and have a good professor, ask him about just where did the stamp comes from that you've seen on many cases. Who put it on the paperwork and who authorized the citation restriction. Just who is tampering with the law?

There is one thing certain, the creditor and or his agents are watching these cases very carefully. The creditor and his agents must balance their books. When you think of the IRS, be aware that the IRS is an agent of the creditor, the corporate International Bankers. This is just one of the Banker's state side agencies.

The General Accounting Office (GAO) is charged with the responsibility to keep track of the debt. All the states have to send reports to Washington, D.C. Then Washington D.C., itself, has to send reports to the GAO. Take a look at your state Comptroller's Annual Report to the Governor of your state.

I found my state's in the library located in the city of the corporate state capital. Look under "Trust Fund" for each state sub-corporation like the state courts, HRS, Banks, Education, etc. you will be amazed at the amount of money being pumped into the Trust Fund from the various Corporate State Department Revenues (all revenue is referred to as taxes, fines, fees, licenses, etc.).

There are millions and billions of your hard earned worthless Federal Reserve Notes, "dollars", being held in "trust." This money is being siphoned off into the coffers of the International Bankers while the corporate government officials are hounding you for more taxes.

All this accounting is not so the people will know what is going on. The accounting reports are for the Banker creditors to keep tabs on just where their collections are coming from. The Bankers want to know if the bankruptcy debt payments are coming in and just how much and from what sources.

This accounting is the purpose behind M1, M2, M3, M4, and M5. All this accounting is closely monitored. Maybe every day, but at least once a week. These M's are the reports of the amounts of money in circulation. The amount of debt out there, and the amount of credit out there. The floating of debt in the form of bonds.

There are five different categories. This system had to come into existence in order for the creditors to be on top of the bankruptcy at all times. This system allows the creditors to figure out and know exactly what is going on in their domain.

It all makes sense. Don't the bankers hire bill collectors? Creditors hire bill collectors to snoop around to see why you're not paying. They want to know how much you are going to pay so they can figure out how much will be coming in. How much will they collect? They want to know who will pay and who won't. The whole system is nothing but credit and debt.

26
Agenda 21: The President's Plans For America

Agenda 21 is a UN document, written in 1992 at the Rio Conference that spells out how the elites who run the UN want us all to live. High density is in. Mass transit is the future. Bike lanes are how we will get to work. Suburbs, rural areas, grass, open space, forests, elbow room are things of the past. Cars and trucks are out. Bikes and trains are in.

But the worst part of Agenda 21 is that the President has bought into it and is promoting it throughout the United States. The elite globalists who run the United Nations are using planning and the Agenda 21 model to restructure our lives and live them according to their — and not our — wishes.

We do not believe that UN black helicopters are on their way to take over our country. But we are convinced that, figuratively, they are on their way as the UN devises strategies to control our lives, tax us, and merge our sovereignty into one-world government.

The President has set up a special task force on rural America, not to improve the lives of those who live there, but to use tax incentives, economic development initiatives, and zoning decisions to herd them into cities whether or not they like it or want to move.

Already, thousands of localities around America have adopted Agenda 21 as the framework for their zoning and land use decisions.

In the name of carbon emission reductions, to avert the theoretical danger of climate change, we are being told to live differently, work differently, and play differently.

Agenda 21 is to the 21st Century what the enclosure acts were to 19th Century Britain, and collectivization was to 20th Century Russia — ways to force people off the land and into the cities.

These earlier schemes were designed to create a work force for the factories of the industrial revolution. These proposals are all aimed at cutting driving, reducing gasoline consumption, and curbing carbon emissions.

Remember how Obama said in his 2007 video that was just unearthed by the Daily Caller, he said "we don't need roads in the suburbs" and called for increased spending for mass transit? He was echoing Agenda 21.

We all need zoning to stop industrial factories from building in residential neighborhoods. We want to use it to preserve historic buildings. Land use decisions are needed to protect wetlands and the environment.

But Agenda 21 carries it too far. It uses government planning to replace the free market system and individual free choice. It uses the power of the state to tell us how to live and where to live. It is a breakthrough to inject the public sector into decisions that are best left to each of us as individuals.

We must oppose Agenda 21 to preserve our freedom. We must be alive to the dangers it poses.

27
Notice of the Bankrupcy

Attn: "Public Servant"

On the night of December 23, 1913, the U.S. Congress committed perhaps the greatest act of treason in history. It surrendered the nation's sovereignty and sold the American people into slavery to a cabal of arch-charlatan bankers who proceeded to plunder, bankrupt, and conquer the nation with a money swindle.

The "money" the banks issue is merely bookkeeping entries. It cost them nothing and is not backed by their wealth, efforts, property, or risk. It is not redeemable except in more debt paper. The Federal Reserve Act forces us to pay compound interest on thin air. We now use worthless "notes", backed by our own credit, that we cannot own, and are made subject to compelled performance for the "privilege" of its use.

From 1913 until 1933 the U.S. paid the "interest" with more and more gold. The structured inevitability soon transpired; the Treasury was empty, the debt was greater than ever, and the U.S. declared bankruptcy. In exchange for using notes owned by the bankers who create them out of nothing on our own credit, we are forced to repay in substance (labor, property, land, businesses, resources - life) in ever-increasing amounts. This may be the greatest swindle, heist and fraud of all time.

When a government goes bankrupt, it looses its sovereignty. In 1933 the U.S. declared bankruptcy, as expressed in Roosevelt's Executive Orders 6073, 6102, 6111, and 6260; House Joint Resolution 192 of June 5, 1933 confirmed in **Perry v. U.S.** (1935) 294 U.S. 330-381, 79 LEd 912, as well as in 31 USC 5112, 5119, and 12 USC 95a. (USC = United States Code.)

The bankrupt U.S. went into receivership, and reorganized in favor of its new owners and creditors, in 1913, and turned over America lock, stock, and barrel to a handful of criminals whose avowed intent, from the beginning, was to plunder, bankrupt, conquer, and enslave the people of the United States of America, and eliminate the nation from the face of the earth. The goal was, and is, to absorb America into a one-world private government and "New World Order."

With the *Erie Railroad v. Thompkins* case of 1938 the Supreme Court confirmed their success. We are now in an international private commercial jurisdiction in colorable admiralty-maritime law, under the Law Merchant. We have been conned and betrayed out of our sovereignty, our rights, our property, our freedom, our common law, Article III courts, and our Republic. The Bill of Rights has been statutized into commercial "civil rights".

America has been stolen. We have been made slaves: permanent debtors, who are bankrupt, in legal incapacity, rendered "commercial persons", "residents", and corporate franchisees known as "citizens of the United States" under the so-called "14th Amendment" which was never ratified. — see Congressional Record, June 13, 1967; *Dyett v. Turner,* (1968) 439 P2d 266, 267; and *State v. Phillips,* (1975).

"You have rights antecedent to all earthly governments; rights that cannot be repealed or restrained by human laws; rights derived from the Great Legislator of the Universe." — *John Adams, Second President of the United States.*

Extreme Plight

28

Notice Letter Instructions and Options

I. Instructions.

This chain letter consists of two aspects:

1. A copy of these "Instructions and Options" and the letter to "Public Servants" should be sent to as many friends and associates as you wish.

2. Send Copies of the "Public Servant" letter (without Instructions) to as many "public servants" as possible. Send to local, State, and Federal governments - police, councilmen, mayors, district attorneys, State and Federal Agencies, Congressman, Senators, judges, lawyers, etc. Anyone in position of "authority."

Send also to the media - newspapers, news magazines, TV, radio, etc. It is important that those in "power" know what they are doing, *and that we know that they know.*

The point of this is to inform Americans of their **extreme plight**. We have no more country. It has been stolen - along with our lives, rights, and property. This is not paranoia, exaggeration, or hyperbole. It is the tragic truth. As a result, all "officials" are either fools or knaves who should no longer be coupled with... or the System considered legitimate.

II. Options

We have been defrauded and conned out of everything

— our rights, freedoms, property, and country. We have the following options:

1. Do Nothing, remain naive-suckers, keep believing the monstrous absurdity that the "government" is our friend, represents us, or we have any ownership of and control over it. In this case we will remain slaves and become ever-increasingly hopeless with each passing instant as our legal entanglements and financial indebtedness grow. The end of this path is ruin.

2. Trust that those in power, who now own and run the world, will have a change of heart, surrender their wealth and power and give our freedom, property, and rights back to us.

3. Expect, hope, or pray for divine intervention (how can we expect God to care and do anything if we don't?)

4. Try to fight our way out. This is an inferior option, as governments, posing as "protectors," have bled their people dry to pay for the greatest assemblage of weapons of destruction in world history, which are now arrayed against us.

5. We can think our way out, wake up from our stupor, take legal/moral measures to withdraw from the System, and not accept any benefits or engage in any involvement with it.

From the "Declaration of Independence" that Thomas Jefferson wrote:

"...whenever any Form of Government becomes destructive of these Ends, it is the Right of the people to alter or to abolish it, and to institute new Government..."

Never has there been a more treacherous and insidious System than that which has conquered this country without Americans even knowing they have been defeated.

No one, however, needs any document or other party to justify his own **"Declaration of Independence"**. Freedom is everyone's innate responsibility and right. Each individual has free will over his own life, and an obligation of stewardship for its care.

What sane man would turn over power to strangers to invent and impose the rules by which he is to be made to live? Moreover, no one has any right to delegate or "vote" for any individuals, or institutions, to exert power over other human beings. Life, death, economy, justice, law, and human fulfillment are at issue. Everyone is consummately justified in questioning the basis of all rules imposed on him.

Suggestions for Action:

1. Read, learn, contact "Patriot" groups for information;

2. Realize that we have been had. Abandon all and every shred of the delusion that the Government is your government, represents your interests, is legitimate, or is anything other than what it actually is: the machinery for administering your permanent conquest, plunder, enslavement, and bankruptcy.

3. Do not pay any taxes.

Every penny you pay in taxes, to your State or to the Federal Government, goes to pay the phony, fraudulent, "National Debt," which is unredeemable. Every cent goes to enrich the insatiable coffers of a group of arch-charlatans who have stolen our country and us along with it.

All taxes go to finance America's subjugation and plunder.

Instead of 1040's or other tax forms send a copy of the "Public Servants" letter, with a blank tax form.

This letter is the result of many years of legal research. What is stated barley scratches the surface. If you wish to know more, the following books can give you a start:

U.S. of A. the Republic - How You Lost It, How You Get It Back! — by Lee Brobst. $15.00 Post-paid. Write: Agro-Bio Systems, POB 1250 Grass Valley, California, 95945;

Conspirator's Hierarchy - The Committee of 300, — by Jack Coleman, 1-800-942-0821;

Secrets of the Federal Reserve (and numerous other books) by Eustace Mullins, Bankers Research Institute, POB 1105, Staunton, Virginia.

29

Research Material to get Copies of:

1. Treaties between the United States and others in Geneva, Switzerland from 1928 to 1932.

2. Minutes of the same meetings, as in No. 1, specifically for the year 1930.

3. The Federal Reserve Act of 1913.

4. House Joint Resolution No. 192 of June 5, 1933.

5. Presidential Executive Orders 6073, 6102, 6111, 6260.

6. 31 USC 5112 and 5119, and 12 USC 95a.

7. Case Law to Copy:

    a. *Erie R.R. v. Thompkins,* (1938)
    b. *Perry v. U.S.,* (1935) 294 U.S. 330-381, 79 LEd 912
    c. *Dyett v. Turner,* (1968) 439 P2d 266, 267
    d. *State of Utah v. Phillips,* 540 P.2d 936 (1975)
    8. *Benedicts on Admiralty*

Investigate the Lawyers Guild of Great Britain and any ties to the American Bar Association.

Extreme Plight

30
Jury Duty

"...That this nation, under God, shall have a new birth of Freedom..." — *Abraham Lincoln.*

Our "Ancient Principles" need to be revived. They refer to the Ten Commandments and the Common Law. The Common Law, in simple terms, is common sense that has its roots in the Ten Commandments.

In 1776 we came out of BONDAGE with FAITH, UNDERSTANDING and COURAGE.

Even against great odds, and with much bloodshed, we battled our way to achieve LIBERTY.

LIBERTY is that delicate balance between the force of government and the FREEWILL of man.

LIBERTY brings FREEDOM of choice to work, to trade, to go and live where one wishes; it leads to ABUNDANCE. But ABUNDANCE, if made an end to itself, will result in COMPLACENCY, which leads to APATHY.

APATHY is the "let George do it" philosophy, which always leads to DEPENDENCY. For a period of time, dependents are often not aware they are dependent. They delude themselves by thinking that they are still free —

"We never had it so good."—"We can still vote, can't we?"

Eventually abundance diminishes and DEPENDENCY becomes known by its true nature: **BONDAGE!**

There are few ways out of bondage. Bloodshed and war often result, but our founding fathers learned of a better way. Realizing that a CREATOR is always above and greater than that which He creates, they established a three vote system by which an informed citizenry can control those acting in the name of the government.

To be a good master you must always remember the true "pecking order" — or chain of command, — in this nation:

1. GOD created man . . .
2. Man (that's you) created the Constitution . . .
3. Constitution created government . . .
4. Government created corporations . .etc.

The base of power was to remain in WE THE PEOPLE but unfortunately, it was lost to those leaders acting in the name of the government, such as politicians, bureaucrats, judges, lawyers, etc.

As a result America is now functioning like a democracy instead of the REPUBLIC it is meant to be.

A democracy is dangerous because it is a one-vote system as opposed to a Republic, which is a three-vote system: Three votes to check tyranny, not just one.

American citizens have not been informed of their other two votes.

Our first vote is at the polls on election-day when we pick those who are to represent us in the seats of government. But what can be done if those elected officials just don't perform as promised or expected? Well, the second two votes are the most effective means by which the common people of any nation on earth have even had in controlling those appointed to serve them in government.

The second vote comes when you serve on a Grand Jury. Before anyone can be brought to trial for a capital or infamous crime by those acting in the name of the government, permission must be obtained from people serving on the Grand Jury!

The Minneapolis Star and Tribune in March 27, 1987, edition noted a purpose of the grand Jury in this way:

"A Grand Jury's purpose is to protect the public from an overzealous prosecutor."

The third is the most powerful vote: this is when you are acting as a jury member yourself during a courtroom trial. At this point, "the buck stops" with you!

It is in this setting that each JUROR has MORE POWER than the President of the United States, all of Congress, and all of the judges combined into one!

Congress can legislate, or "make law", the President or some other bureaucrat can make orders, or issue regulations, and judges may make a decision, or instruct, but no JUROR can ever be punished for voting "Not Guilty!"

Any juror can, with complete impunity, choose to disregard the instructions of any judge or attorney in rendering his vote. If only one JUROR should vote "Not Guilty" for any reason, there is no conviction and no punishment for the accused, at the end of the trial.

Thus, those acting in the name of government must come before the common man to get his permission to enforce law.

Extreme Plight

31
You Are Above The Law

As a JUROR in a trial setting, when it comes to your individual vote of innocent or guilty, you are truly only answerable to ALMIGHTY GOD.

The First Amendment to the Constitution was born out of this great concept. However, many judges of today refuse to inform JURORS of their RIGHTS.

THe Minneapolis Star and Tribune in a news paper article appearing in its November 30, 1984 edition, entitled: "What Judges Don't Tell Juries" stated:

"At the time of adoption of the Constitution, the jury's role, as a defense against political oppression, was unquestioned in American jurisprudence. This nation survived until the 1850's, when prosecutions under the Fugitive Slave Act were largely unsuccessful because juries refused to convict the accused."

"Then judges began to erode the institution of free juries, leading to the absurd compromise that is the current state of the law. While our courts uniformly state that juries have the power to return a verdict of not guilty, whatever the facts my be, they routinely tell jurors just the opposite."

"Furthermore, the courts will not allow the defendants or their counsel to inform the jurors of their true power. Any lawyer who made . . . Hamilton's argument would face professional discipline and charges of contempt of court."

"By what logic should juries have the power to acquit a defendant, but no right to know about that power? Court decisions that have suppressed the notion of **jury nullification** cannot resolve this paradox."

"More than logic has suffered. As originally conceived, juries were to be made **a safety valve way** to soften the bureaucratic rigidity of the judicial system by introducing the community's common sense."

"If they are to function effectively as the 'conscience of the community,' jurors must be told that they have the power **and the right** to say no to a prosecution in order to achieve a greater good. To cut jurors off from this information is to undermine one of our most important institutions."

The community should educate itself. Then citizens called for jury duty could teach the judges a needed lesson in civics. One of the important ways our nation's founders provided to insure that *you* — not the growing army of politicians, judges, lawyers, and bureaucrats — *rule this nation.*

The lesson focuses on *the rule of power you possess* as a JUROR, how you got it, why you have it, and remind you of the basis on which you must decide not only the facts placed in evidence but also the validity and applicability of every law, rule, regulation, ordinance, or instruction given by any man seated as a judge or attorney when you serve as a JUROR.

One JUROR can stop tyranny with a "NOT GUILTILY VOTE!" He can nullify bad law in any case, by **"HANGING THE JURY!"**

The only power the judge has over the JURY is their ignorance!

32
Jury Rights

"**The jury has the right to judge both the law as well as the fact in controversy.**" — *John Jay, 1st Chief Justice U.S. supreme Court, 1789.*

"**The jury has the right to determine both the law and the facts.**" — *Samuel Chase, U.S. supreme Court Justice, 1796, Signer of the unanimous Declaration.*

"**The jury has the power to bring a verdict in the teeth of both law and fact.**" — *Oliver Wendell Holmes, U.S. supreme Court Justice, 1902.*

"**The law itself is on trial, quite as much as the cause which is to be decided.**" — *Harlan F. Stone, 12th Chief Justice U.S. supreme Court, 1941.*

"**The pages of history shine on instances of the jury's exercise of its prerogative to disregard instructions of the judge...**" — *U.S. vs. Dougherty, 473 F 2nd 1113, 1139. (1972).*

Extreme Plight

33
Trial by Jury

• **JURY TAMPERING?** A JURY's Rights, Powers and Duties:

The Charge to the JURY in the first JURY Trial before the supreme Court of the U.S. Illustrates the TRUE POWER OF THE JURY.

In the February term of 1794, the supreme Court conducted a JURY trial and said:

"It is presumed that the juries are the best judges of facts; it is, on the other hand, presumed that the courts are the best judges of law. But still both objects are within our power of decision."

"You have a right to take upon yourselves to judge of both, and to determine the <u>law</u> as well as the <u>fact</u> in controversy." — *State of Georgia vs. Brailsford, et al, 3 Dall. 1.*

"The JURY has an unreviewable and unreversible power . . . to acquit in disregard of the instructions on the law given by the trial judge . . ." — *(emphasis added) U.S. vs. Dougherty, 473 F 2nd 1113, 1139 (1972).*

Hence, **JURY disregard** of the limited and generally conviction-oriented evidence presented for its consideration, and **JURY disregard** for what the trial judge wants them to believe is the controlling law in the particular case (sometimes called **JURY lawlessness**) is not something to be scrupulously avoided, but rather encouraged.

Witness the following quotation from the eminent legal authority above-mentioned:

"Jury lawlessness is the greatest corrective of law in its actual administration. The will of the state at large imposed on a reluctant community, and the will of a majority imposed on a vigorous and determined minority, find the same obstacle in the local JURY that formerly confronted ministers and kings." *(emphasis added) (Dougherty cited above, note 32 at 1130).*

The word 'Supreme' is not capitalized in the Constitution, however Behavior is.

Jury lawlessness means willingness to nullify bad law.

• RIGHT OF THE JURY TO BE TOLD ITS POWER

Almost every JURY in the land is falsely instructed by the judge when it is told it must accept as the law that which is given to them by the court, and that the JURY can decide only the facts of the case. This is to destroy the purpose of a Common Law JURY, and to permit the imposition of tyranny upon a people.

"There is nothing more terrifying than ignorance in action." — *Goethe (engraved on a plaque at the Naval War College).*

"To embarrass justice by a multiplicity of laws, or to hazard it by confidence in judges, are the opposite rocks on which all civil instructions have been

wrecked." — *Johnson (engraved in Minnesota State Capitol Outside the Supreme Court Chambers)*

"The letter killeth, but the spirit giveth life." — *II Corinthians 3:6*

"It is error alone which needs the support of government. truth can stand by itself." — *Thomas Jefferson*

The JURY'S options are by no means limited to the choices presented to it in the courtroom.

"The jury gets its understanding as to the arrangements in the legal system from more than one voice. There is the formal communication from the 'judge.' There is informal communication from the total culture — literature; current comment, conversation; and, of course, history and tradition." — *Dougherty cited above, at 1135.*

• LAWS, FACTS, AND EVIDENCE

Without the power to decide what facts, law and evidence are applicable, JURIES cannot be a protection to the accused. If people acting in the name of government are permitted by JURORS to dictate any law whatever, they can also unfairly dictate what evidence is admissible or inadmissible and thereby prevent the WHOLE TRUTH from being considered.

Thus if government can manipulate and control both the law and the evidence, the issue of fact becomes virtually irrelevant. In reality, true JUSTICE would be denied leaving us with a trial by government and not a trial by JURY!

• HOW DOES TYRANNY BEGIN? WHY ARE THERE SO MANY LAWS?

Heroes are men of glory who are so honored because of some heroic deed. People often out of gratitude yield allegiance to them. Honor and allegiance are nice words for power! Power and allegiance can only be held rightfully by trust as a result of continued character.

When people acting in the name of government violate ethics, they break trust with "WE THE PEOPLE." The natural result is for "WE THE PEOPLE" to pull back power (honor and allegiance).

The loss of power creates fear for those losing the power. Fearing loss of power, people acting in the name of government often seek to regain or at least hold their power. Hence, to legitimize their quest for control, laws and force are often instituted.

Unchecked power is the foundation of tyranny. It is the JUROR'S duty to use the JURY ROOM as a vehicle to stem the tide of oppression and tyranny: To prevent bloodshed by peacefully removing power from those who have abused it. The JURY is the primary vehicle for peaceful restoration of LIBERTY, POWER AND HONOR TO "WE THE PEOPLE!"

34
Law of the Land

The general misconception is that any statute passed by legislators bearing the appearance of law constitutes the law of the land. The U.S. Constitution is the supreme law of the land, and any statute, to be valid, must be in agreement.

It is impossible for a law, which violates the Constitution to be valid. This is succinctly stated as follows:

"All laws which are repugnant to the Constitution are null and void." — *Marbury vs. Madison, 5 US (2 Cranch) 137, 174, 176, (1803).*

"When rights secured by the Constitution are involved, there can be no rule making or legislation which would abrogate them." — *Miranda vs. Arizona, 384 US 436 p. 491.*

"An unconstitutional act is not law; it confers no rights; it imposes no duties; affords no protection; it creates no office; it is in legal contemplation, as inoperative as though it had never been passed." — *Norton vs. Shelby County 118 US 425 p. 442.*

"The general rule is that an unconstitutional statute, though having the form and name of law, is in reality no law, but is wholly void, and ineffective for any

purpose; since unconstitutionality dates from the time of its enactment, and not merely from the date of the decision so branding it.

No one is bound to obey an unconstitutional law and no courts are bound to enforce it." — *16 Am Jur 2nd, Sec 177 late 2d, Sec 256.*

35

Summary of the Ten Commandments

The TEN COMMANDMENTS represent GOD'S GOVERNMENT OVER MAN! GOD commands us for our own good to give up wrongs; and not our rights! HIS system always results in FREEDOM and LIBERTY! The Constitution and the Bill of Rights are built on this foundation, which provides for punitive justice. It is not until one damages another persons property that he can be punished.

The Marxist system leads to bondage, and GOD'S system leads to LIBERTY!

Read very carefully:

1. Thou shalt have no other gods before Me.
2. Thou shalt not make unto thee any graven image.
3. Thou shalt not take the name of the Lord thy God in vain.
4. Remember the Sabbath to keep it Holy.
5. Honor thy father and thy mother.
6. Thou shalt not murder.
7. Thou shalt not commit adultery.
8. Thou shalt not steal.
9. Thou shalt not bear false witness.
10. Thou shalt not covet.

Directly above the Chief Justice's chair is a tablet signifying the TEN COMMANDMENTS. When the Speaker of the House in the U.S. Congress looks up, his eyes look into the face of Moses.

"The Bible is the Book upon which this Republic rests." — *Andrew Jackson, Seventh President of the United States.*

"The moral principles and precepts contained in the Scriptures ought to form the basis of all our civil constitutions and laws. All the miseries and evils which men suffer from vice, crime, ambition, injustice, oppression, slavery, and war, proceed from their despising or neglecting the precepts of the Bible." — *Noah Webster*

36

Summary of the Communist Manifesto

The Communist Manifesto represents a misguided philosophy, which teaches the citizens to give up their RIGHTS for the sake of the "common good," but it always ends in a police state.

This is called preventive justice.

Control is the key concept. Read carefully:

1. Abolition of private property.

2. Heavy progressive income tax.

3. Abolition of all rights on inheritance.

4. Confiscation of property of all emigrants and rebels.

5. Central bank.

6. Government control of Communications & Transportation.

7. Government ownership of factories and agriculture.

8. Government control of labor.

9. Corporate farms, regional planning.

10. Government control of education.

GIVE UP RIGHTS FOR THE "COMMON GOOD"?

Where people fear the government you have tyranny; where the government fears the people, you have liberty.

Politicians, bureaucrats and especially judges would have you believe that too much freedom will result in chaos. Therefore, we should gladly give up some of our RIGHTS for the good of the community.

In other words, people acting in the name of the government, say we need *more laws* and more JURORS to enforce these laws — even if we have to give up some RIGHTS in the process. They believe the more laws we have, the more control, thus a better society.

This theory may sound good on paper, and apparently many of our leaders think this way, as evidenced by the thousands of new laws that are added to the books each year in this country. But, no matter how cleverly this Marxist argument is made, the hard fact is that whenever you give up a RIGHT you lose a "FREE CHOICE"!

This adds another control. Control's real name is BONDAGE! The logical conclusion would be, if giving up some RIGHTS produces a better society, then by giving up all RIGHTS we could produce a perfect society.

We could chain everybody to a tree, for lack of TRUST. This may prevent crime, but it would destroy PRIVACY, which is the heartbeat of FREEDOM! It would also destroy TRUST which is the foundation for DIGNITY. Rather than giving up RIGHTS, we should be giving up wrongs!

The opposite of control is not chaos. More laws do not make less criminals! We must give up wrongs, not rights, for a better society!

"Necessity is the plea for every infringement of human liberty; it is the argument of tyrants; it is the creed of slaves." — *William Pitt of the British House of Commons.*

37

Inalienable [Unalienable] or Natural Rights

NATURAL RIGHTS ARE THOSE RIGHTS such as life (from conception), LIBERTY and the PURSUIT OF HAPPINESS, e.g. FREEDOM OF RELIGION, SPEECH, LEARNING, TRAVEL, SELF-DEFENSE, POSESSION OF PROPERTY, ETC.

Hence laws and statutes which violate NATURAL RIGHTS, though they may have the color of law, are not law but impostors! The U.S. Constitution was written to protect these NATURAL RIGHTS from being tampered with by legislators.

Our forefathers also wisely knew that the U.S. Constitution would be utterly worthless to restrain government legislators unless it was clearly understood that the people had the right to compel the government to keep within the Constitutional limits.

Lysander Spooner wrote as follows:

"Government is established for the protection of the weak against the strong. This is the principal, if not the sole motive for the establishment of all legitimate government. It is only the weaker party who loses their liberties, when a government becomes oppressive. The stronger party, in all governments are free by virtue of their superior strength.

They never oppress themselves.

Legislation is the work of the stronger party; and if, in addition to the sole power of legislation, they have the sole power of determining what legislation shall be enforced, they have all power in their hands, and the weaker party are the subjects of an absolute government.

Unless the weaker party have veto, they have no power whatever in the government . . . no liberties . . .

The trial by jury is the only institution that gives the weaker party any veto upon the power of the stronger. Consequently it is the only institution that gives them any effective voice in the government, or any guaranty against tyrannical oppression.

Rights come from GOD; not from the State!

Extreme Plight

Appendix

Extreme Plight

Please Take Note

If Frank Brushaber was a **nonresident alien** with respect to **the federal zone,** then so am I, and so are millions of other Americans, who will know the truth if We teach them.

Before the 14th Amendment, adopted in 1868:

... For it is certain, that in the sense in which the word "Citizen" is used in the federal Constitution, "Citizen of each State," and "Citizen of the United States," are convertible terms; **_they mean the same thing;_** for "the Citizens of each State are entitled to all Privileges and Immunities of Citizens in the several States," and "Citizens of the United States" are, of course, Citizens of all the United States.

[*44 Maine 518 (1859), Hathaway, J. dissenting*]

After the 14th Amendment, adopted in 1868:

It is quite clear, then, that there is a citizenship of the United States [Inc.] and a citizenship of a State, which are **_distinct from each other_** and which depend upon different characteristics or circumstances in the individual.

[*Slaughter House Cases, 83 U.S. 36 (1873)*]

The first clause of the fourteenth amendment made negroes citizens of the United States [Inc.] and citizens of the State in which they reside, and thereby created **_two classes of citizens,_** one of the United States [Inc.] and the other of the State.

[*Cory et al. v. Carter, 48 Ind. 327 (1874) headnote 8*]

We have in our political system a Government of the United States [Inc.] and a government of each of the several States. Each one of these governments is distinct from the others, and **each has citizens of its own** ....

[*U.S. v. Cruikshank, 92 U.S. 542 (1875)*]

One may be a citizen of a State and yet Not a citizen of the United States [Inc.].

[*Thomasson v. State, 15 Ind. 449; Cory v. Carter, 48 Ind. 327 (17 Am. R. 738); McCarthy v. Froelke, 63 Ind. 507; In Re Wehlitz, 16 Wis. 443; McDonel v. State, 90 Ind. 320, 323 (1883)*]

"You have the Right to remain silent"

"And the Chief Priests accused Jesus of many things: but he answered them nothing.

And Pilate asked him again saying, 'Answereth thou nothing?' Behold how many things they witness against thee.

But Jesus yet answered nothing; so Pilate marveled." — Mark 15:3-5

Jesus, at his trial before the Court of Pilate, said nothing. He stood mute. The record shows that this act was so unusual, so wise, that the Judge of His case *"marveled"*. The Greek word used here is *"thaumazo"* meaning, by implication, to admire.

Have you ever wondered about that, this curious marveling by Pilate? You see, Jesus refused to testify into Pilate's *jurisdiction!*

Yet, there are Christians today, when compelled into court, who seem to be prone to keep talking, until by their very words, there is enough evidence admitted into the record to convict them without any further witnesses.

Did you know that 90% of all convictions are obtained by admissions and confessions, generally unwittingly obtained from the defendant himself? It is almost an axiom of law that all of the evidence that will ever be used against a defendant will be furnished by the defendant himself.

This is why the government and local police investigators do all they can to get you to talk to them about the case, giving them your side of the story. Even if you are innocent, your words, uttered during the frustration of being incarcerated and not knowing what will happen next, may be pieced together to frame up a case against you.

Therefore, when you are in custody of the police or federal agents of any kind, do not make any statements or answer any questions, even as to the weather or where you live.

You are to stand mute, say nothing, and keep your mouth shut on any and all subjects. Do not demand a lawyer or permit yourself to be released on bond, for in so doing you may grant them jurisdiction that they might not otherwise have, and thereby forfeit one of your rights under the Common Law.

Stand mute even though you are threatened with contempt of court or even if you think you can answer the questions to your legal advantage. The very first question from the judge that you answer, even to make a plea of "not guilty," is an admission that this court has jurisdiction over you.

Jurisdiction is a legal point of law that must be determined by the court **before** it can move forward with your case. If that cannot be proven, the case must be dismissed. Therefore, **why volunteer** to prove that point for them by answering questions of the court?

Further, if you answer as to how you plead, you not only admit to jurisdiction, but you admit to **"understanding"** [**"standing under"**] the charges that have been placed against you, and that you are therefore mentally competent to stand trial.

Remember the Chief Priests in their black robes are not going to appreciate what we have instructed you in these few paragraphs. They want you to make **admissions**, even that you are "not guilty", so that they can establish **jurisdiction** over your person. They want you to **volunteer** evidence, such as fingerprints and photographs, without counsel of your choice being present.

They are professionals at the use of words, fears, anxieties and threats to trick you into giving the **admissions** and **confessions** they really need to get a conviction.

The problem is that you **assume** that you are innocent until proven guilty, or that they will accept your simple explanation and drop the whole thing. Don't be so naive or take such a chance with your future.

Stand mute, as Christ taught us, and even maybe the court will "marvel."

Extreme Plight

The 545 People Responsible for all of America's Woes

Politicians are the only people in the world who create problems and then campaign against them.

Have you ever wondered why, if both the Democrats and the Republicans are against deficits, we have deficits? Have you ever wondered why, if all the politicians are against inflation and high taxes, we have inflation and high taxes?

You and I don't propose a federal budget. The president does. You and I don't have the Constitutional authority to vote on appropriations. The House of Representatives does. You and I don't write the tax code. Congress does. You and I don't set fiscal policy. Congress does. You and I don't control monetary policy. The Federal Reserve Bank does.

One hundred senators, 435 congressmen, one president and nine Supreme Court justices - 545 human beings out of the 235 million - are directly, legally, morally and individually responsible for the domestic problems that plague this country.

I excluded the members of the Federal Reserve Board because that problem was created by the Congress. In 1913, Congress delegated its Constitutional duty to provide a sound currency to a federally chartered but private central bank.

I excluded the special interests and lobbyists for a sound reason. They have no legal authority. They have no ability to coerce a senator, a congressman or a president to do one cotton-picking thing. I don't care if they offer a politician $1 million dollars in cash. The politician has the power to accept or reject it.

No matter what the lobbyist promises, it is the legislation's responsibility to determine how he votes.

A CONFIDENCE CONSPIRACY

Don't you see how the con game that is played on the people by the politicians? Those 545 human beings spend much of their energy convincing you that what they did is not their fault. They cooperate in this common con regardless of party.

What separates a politician from a normal human being is an excessive amount of gall. No normal human being would have the gall of Tip O'Neill, who stood up and criticized Ronald Reagan for creating deficits.

The president can only propose a budget. He cannot force the Congress to accept it. The Constitution, which is the supreme law of the land, gives sole responsibility to the House of Representatives for originating appropriations and taxes.

The speaker of the House is the leader of the majority party. He and his fellow Democrats, not the president, can approve any budget they want. If the president vetos it, they can pass it over his veto.

REPLACE SCOUNDRELS

It seems inconceivable to me that a nation of 235 million cannot replace 545 people who stand convicted — by present facts — of incompetence and irresponsibility.

I can't think of a single domestic problem, from an unfair tax code to defense overruns, that is not traceable directly to those 545 people.

When you fully grasp the plain truth that 545 people exercise power of the federal government, then it must follow that what exists is what they want to exist.

If the tax code is unfair, it's because they want it unfair. If the budget is in the red, it's because they want it in the red. If the Marines are in Afganistan, it's because they want them in Afganistan.

There are no insoluble government problems. Do not let these 545 people shift the blame to bureaucrats, whom they hire and whose jobs they can abolish; to lobbyists, whose gifts and advice they can reject; to regulators, to whom they give the power to regulate and from whom they can take it.

Above all, do not let them con you into the belief that there exist disembodied mystical forces like "the economy," "inflation" or "politics" that prevent them from doing what they take an oath to do.

Those 545 people and they alone are responsible. They and they alone have the power. They and they alone should be held accountable by the people who are their bosses — provided their bosses have the guts to manage their own employees.

Extreme Plight

Major Changes Ahead

We are in a time of great change. **America's *Currency* was captured in 1913, and America's *Government* was captured in 1933.** This explains why petitioning our government for grievances has been to no meaningful avail.

Corporations that masquerade as our lawful government today, have almost *destroyed* America! Top people in our government — *including our military* — know this. They have been waiting for the "right time" to help *take America back to our lawful government.*

In the very near future, we can expect a major constructive change in our banking and currency system. We can expect to see contingents of Federal Marshals acting in the major seats of power — backed up by our Military.

These Military people are NOT any part of a military coup. They are backing up the Civilian re-establishment of our lost, lawful, government.

We can expect to see minor inter-ruptions in our normal way of life.

This Transition has been designed to minimize interruptions in vital services in our economy — to minimize hardship.

This Transition will be accompanied by announcements in mainstream media. What we do *not* want is for people to become alarmed.

Our *so-called* "president" has been informed that he is *no longer* the Commander in Chief of our Military!

This is part of a worldwide operation whereby the non-aligned nations — *those nations that are not part of the G20* — will re-establish solid currencies.

There will be additional announce-ments to come — designed to slowly awaken the masses; to reduce panic.

Civil authority has been restored to the people. The Military, who exist only through Civil authority, will be ready to assist the People whom they are sworn to protect in the effort to restore this nation to the Constitutional Republic it was created to be.

International Law has been unlawfully in effect in America since 1933. And *rescinding this law,* has been on the table since the 1950s.

We the People have regained Civilian Authority, in order to use the Military Services to support the ongoing effort to bring us back to true government "of, for and by the people".

Do *not* misread what is going on — they are *NOT* coming for the People. **The Cabal's time is up!**

Please prepare for *"good"* changes to come.

Please share this information with others. The foundation has been laid. All that is needed now is YOU! — regular, everyday people will be needed for their insight, opinions and voice.

PLEASE SHARE THIS INFORMATION; EVERY AMERICAN MUST HEAR THIS, TO KNOW WHAT IS HAPPENING!

Declaration to the World

Just before the end of last year, Pennsylvania — *as a state* — removed itself from the RuSA organization. After they did this, they put together a **Declaration of Notice to the World** stating that the Commonwealth of Pennsylvania had returned itself and its people back under its *de jur* Constitution, *of the 1700s,* and declared the People of Pennsylvania, Free! — no longer recognizing *unlawful corporate govern-ment* within their state.

They did this *legally and properly.* They did not ask for permission, they simply went ahead and did it. And they received their receipt back from the Office of Private International Law at the Hague.

And shortly after that, an informed contact — who had been in touch with the various groups who had come forward in the beginning, concerning funding for RuSA and Rap, before changes were made and they withdrew their support —was contacted and given a simple message, and that message was this:

"It has come to our attention, what Pennsylvania has done. How long would it take you to put together a simple majority of states to duplicate what Pennsylvania has done, for at such a time there could be monetary and military support?"

They asked for a copy of the original documentation that Pennsylvania had submitted to the Office of Private International Law at the Hague, *so they could see who had been involved.*

Our contact had no problem with that, and neither did Pennsylvania. So they forwarded on the documentation that Pennsylvania had submitted. The answer was *"Yes! we'll just see how fast we can get that done!"*

So they sent out emails to everyone across the country that they knew, and had worked with all this time, that they knew to be capable, honorable, and honest Patriots, who would roll up their sleeves and actually get the job done, once they were told what had to be done.

And by the following day, at least one contact in 20-22 states had stepped up and volunteered to be a lead person in their state, to get it done!

The goal was for at least a simple majority — meaning 26 or more states to duplicate *exactly* what Pennsylvania had done.

It was later decided by those involved, to add *more strength* to the action by making the **Declaration of Notice to the World,** collectively as a united effort, so that the world will know we are not just free people in the various free states, but a Free People, *united as we were meant to be.*

We need no permission, recognition or opinion from foreign bodies or corporations to be what we are — Americans who claim our rightful heritage that was given to us by our founders in 1776.

This action should be seen as a *Declaration;* not just a notification — this is primary.

This action is interim; and we can't emphasize that enough.

A small group of elite people, have already screwed things up — and in order to make sure that this doesn't happen again, all of the temporary aspects of this will be in writing.

After a period of about 120 days, free elections will be held. Paper ballots only; machines can be played with; paper ballots are a lot more difficult.

We've been told that old money people from before the Revolutionary War have been in contact with our military, and that some 80-90% of the military agree with the ideology found in our founding documents.

Everything we do is based on the principles in our 1787 Constitution and the Bill of Rights — including the *original 13th Amendment* that prohibits any foreign association, title of nobility, etc. — and the Oath of Service that everybody must take to *"support and defend the Constitution of the United States against all enemies, foreign and domestic."*

The U.S. Military has indicated to the financial people that they are willing to back us and that we have their recognition and support.

This gives the Military — *probably for the first time* — power to be used as a backup to federal Marshals who will take into custody all of the crooks and "fun-and-games people" on Wall Street, and so forth. There is going to be a tremendous house-cleaning.

The reorganizational portions of the government itself should be concluded in about 120 days. This 120 day period will begin with a formal announcement from the press-room of the White House.

This will give every reporter a clean shot at broadcasting the transition.

So these measures — *in terms of what the military wants* — they want to be the good guys. They're tired of being the bad guys. They would much rather be invited into a foreign country as a friend, and an assistant.

You need some help? What do you need? Manpower? Bull-dozers? Food? We can come in and help you out.

Yes! we're the United States Military! but we're the *new* one. We're the good guys. BINGO!

We think this new approach will work quite well.

We are not putting together any interim government. We are not trying to overthrow anything. We are trying to revert back to law and order, and create the smallest amount of chaos, *in the most peaceful fashion that we can*.

Our military cannot do this on their own for the simple reason that under the current structure, Obama is considered to be the President — *we all know that he is not* — he is the CEO (Chief Executive Officer) of a Corporation called THE UNITED STATES.

The majority of the American people do not understand this.

So as long as the American people recognize a criminal corporation in Washington D.C. as having jurisdiction over them — *and they do not stand up and say otherwise* — our military's hands are somewhat tied. They have been taking orders from a fake Commander in Chief.

As far as the financial people are concerned, they will never bring forth the money that's been intended for this country, these many years, until Washington is cleaned out, because if they did, it would disappear down the black hole of theft, almost immediately.

If the military are to once again take their orders from we the people, we have to be ready with a list of what we require it to do.

As pointed out above, this is temporary, and what gives the people the power and the authority and the standing to do this is simply that a majority of states filed the same paperwork that Pennsylvania filed, putting the world on Notice that they have gone back under their *de jur* Constitution.

They have reclaimed the Articles of Confederation, which have never been rescinded.

The Declaration of Independence and the Articles of Confederation are the basis of our freedom.

These arrests will mean the removal of the final obstacles that will allow for the implementation of the *new abundance systems* that are ready to free humanity from the current economy and its falsely imposed conditions of poverty and debt.

There are many men and women dedicated to this cause who have been working diligently in secret for years to bring us to this moment, who are eager to present to humanity the new system that will redistribute abundance to all, and release humanity from the mundane life it has known.

Freedom is being returned to the people.

The release of withheld technologies and other suppressed elements will follow to assist this transition.

The news of these mass arrests will come sudden and come hard, and many who are unprepared with an understand-ing as to why, may feel shocked and confused to see so many people taken into custody.

These people , how ever, have served to perpetuate our enslavement, and all have actively taken part in serious crimes against the people.

Certain big media groups have agreed to cover these events and assist in the disclosure timeline.

These arrests will be televised and fully shared with you, for it is owed to the people of the world that they witness the very moments and actions taken that will mean our release from the control of these people who have for so long worked to exploit and control humanity.

This manipulation will end and all humanity will enter into a new life. True freedom is to be soon returned to you.

"We the People are the rightful master of both congress and the courts — not to overthrow the Constitution, but to overthrow the men who pervert the Constitution."

Extreme Plight

"Silence can only be equated with fraud when there is a legal or moral duty to speak, or when an inquiry left unanswered would be intentionally misleading... We cannot condone this shocking conduct... If that is the case we hope our message is clear. This sort of deception will not be tolerated and if this is routine it should be immediately corrected" — *U.S. v. Tweel 550 F2d 297, 299-300.*

Extreme Plight

Other Publications

1. **Nesara I**
   https://www.createspace.com/3676730
2. **Nesara II**
   https://www.createspace.com/3694967
3. **Be The One**
   https://www.createspace.com/3921716
4. **Commercial Redemption**
   https://www.createspace.com/3397150
5. **Hardcore Redemption-in-Law**
   https://www.createspace.com/3475497
6. **Commercial Law Applied**
   https://www.createspace.com/3960715
7. **The Matrix As It Is**
   https://www.createspace.com/3495158
8. **Give Yourself Credit**
   https://www.createspace.com/3462990
9. **From Debt To Prosperity**
   https://www.createspace.com/3485734
10. **DebtOcracy**
    https://www.createspace.com/3650756
11. **Asset Protection**
    https://www.createspace.com/3700522
12. **Untold History Of America**
    https://www.createspace.com/3407070
13. **New Beginning Study Course**
    https://www.createspace.com/3412422
14. **Reclaim Your Sovereignty**
    https://www.createspace.com/3418256
15. **Oil Beneath Our Feet**
    https://www.createspace.com/3420496
16. **The People's Voice**
    https://www.createspace.com/3724222
17. **My Home Is My Castle**
    https://www.createspace.com/3464566
18. **Maine Street Miracle**
    https://www.createspace.com/3397262

www.ingramcontent.com/pod-product-compliance
Lightning Source LLC
Chambersburg PA
CBHW072308290526
45794CB00002B/569